Dhaka Dust

Dhaka Dust

Poems

Dilruba Ahmed

Graywolf Press

This publication is made possible by funding provided in part by a grant from the Minnesota State Arts Board, through an appropriation by the Minnesota State Legislature, a grant from the National Endowment for the Arts, and private funders. Significant support has also been provided by Target; the McKnight Foundation; and other generous contributions from foundations, corporations, and individuals. To these organizations and individuals we offer our heartfelt thanks.

Published by Graywolf Press
250 Third Avenue North, Suite 600
Minneapolis, Minnesota 55401

www.graywolfpress.org

Published in the United States of America

ISBN 978-1-55597-589-0

2 4 6 8 9 7 5 3 1
First Graywolf Printing, 2011

Library of Congress Control Number: 2011923188

Cover design: Jeenee Lee Design

Cover art: Samina Islam, *Attraction*, www.saminaislam.com

For my mother and my father

For S and K

Contents

Introduction by Arthur Sze   /   ix

Dhaka Dust   /   5

~ I ~

From the Fatwa Series   /   9
Thinking of His Jaywalking Ticket While Boarding
   a Plane at SFO   /   10
What the Fortune Teller Said   /   12
Voltage   /   13
Mississippi Delta   /   15
Dear Masoom   /   16
Halloween   /   18
Dhaka Bazaar before Departure   /   19
The Other Side   /   21
After the Argument   /   22
Small House   /   23
Overheard   /   25
Advice   /   26
Fugue of New Motherhood   /   28
Grace   /   30
Roulade   /   32
Alpana   /   33
Invitation   /   35
Petition   /   38
Ghazal   /   39

~ II ~

Southeastern Ohio   /   43
Turn   /   44
Rumor Had It   /   45
Clepsydra   /   46

Lightning / 47

Clear Water / 48

Amateur's Guide to Divination / 49

Carnival / 50

Picasso's *Self-Portrait in Blue Period,* 1901 / 51

Dustcover / 52

Qawwali / 54

Fever / 56

Josiah / 57

Dust and Ashes / 59

The Gardener's Concession / 60

Return / 62

Witching Hour / 63

~ III ~

Fable / 67

The 18th-Century Weavers of Muslin Whose
Thumbs Were Chopped / 68

Cathedral / 70

At the Stove-Side / 71

Mother / 72

The Map of Another Country / 73

New Year / 74

In Brussels I Learn to Love / 75

Venice during an Election Year in the US / 77

Limoni / 78

Jinn / 79

Evening in Mendocino / 81

Looking for Astronauts / 82

Slicing It Open / 83

In the Echo Chamber / 84

Solstice / 85

Translating Tagore / 87

Dust Catcher / 88

Jackfruit / 89

Introduction

Set in Bangladesh, the opening poem to Dilruba Ahmed's *Dhaka Dust* plunges a reader into a street scene:

> ... rickshaws
> five or six abreast. They are all here:
> studded metal backboards ablaze with red flowers,
>
> Heineken boxes, a Bangladeshi star with blue eyes. ...

Imbued with vivid descriptions and textures, the poem moves by tonal shifts to a continental image of loss:

> the ocean's giant tongue has swept away
> miles of coastline, and bodies flood the water.
>
> Dust sifts into your lungs and sinks—feline,
> black, to remain long after you leave.

The image of dust occurs fifteen times through the book, and, as an image of life's grittiness and impermanence, it grounds the journeys and transformations of the poems in an intensely physical way. At the outset, "a woman breathes into her green shawl / against the dust on the road's median." Later on, at her father's village, relatives "heave a dusty album." A merchant has a pyramid of cinnamon, and his lips are laced with "sweet dust." In other poems, it is dust that makes someone wheeze, or dust that winter winds bring in. The dust can be personified into "a stranger at my door—a pillar / of dust," and it can trigger the memory of a mother in the "mingled scents / of pepper dust and pine." At the end, in a last glimpse of Dhaka, "bikes churn up dust," and the image of the world in ceaseless motion, change, and transformation hangs in the air.

If the poems in this collection shift location easily, from Bangladesh to America to Europe and back to America, the poems also shift perspectives fluidly and use hybridization—cultural location and dislocation—to create a rich and luminous weave. The speaker purchases glass bangles at a Dhaka bazaar before returning to America, but the people there haunt her, and when the speaker says—

> I'm empty-handed.
> I can forget what I've heard and seen,
> I can free myself from this glass.

—the speaker may have nothing in her hands, but she is still wearing the bangles around her wrists. And although she asserts that she can take them off, she has yet to do so.

Rich in implication, the image of the bangles is reiterated in "Overheard," where a thief tries to grab bangles off a sister's arm through an open window:

> He must have seen her bangles
> flash. I clutched the long thick braid
> of her hair after that. Night after
> night, it was a bristled rope to keep
> me from the underworld.

In a lovely surprise, the speaker of the poem attaches herself, not to the bangles, but to her sister's hair to stay suspended and alive in the world. These unexpected, visionary twists empower the poems again and again, and they burst through, at unexpected points, in the scenes of family, motherhood, and domestic life.

In addition to writing with generosity of spirit and verve, Ahmed displays a keen attention to sound and language. Phrases from Bengali, Spanish, Italian, and French interlace the poems in English and are never decorative or forced. They are part of the essential motion of the speaker, who revels in braiding different tongues. In "Translating Tagore," there's a passionate commitment to the physicality of language:

lips
pursed around the plush sounds—

each poem possessing
            your body while every word
        caught in my throat
like a *cattah*.

Been speaking in tongues again.

            In sleep, I read the twists
and turns of text, a curlicued Braille,

tracing membrane pages and thinking
        this is where it says
                there was a boy with a name like a fruit,

or *her eyes were the color of tamarind.*

Clear, sensuous, and astute, Ahmed's poems play and radiate off
each other in subtle and provocative ways. She embraces life in all its
complexity and handles a variety of forms with originality and grace.
And the themes of departures and arrivals, of cultural and poetic
hybridity, resonate gorgeously through this book. Ahmed writes with
her nerves, and she has written herself into existence.

Arthur Sze

Dhaka Dust

When on Route 80 in Ohio
I came across an exit
to Calcutta . . . .

. . . .

The signs to Route 80
all have disappeared . . .

—*Agha Shahid Ali*

Continent, city, country, society:
the choice is never wide and never free.
And here, or there . . . No. Should we have stayed at home,
wherever that may be?

—*Elizabeth Bishop*

Dhaka Dust

Can't occupy the same space at the same time
unless, of course, you land in Dhaka, rickshaws

five or six abreast. They are all here:
studded metal backboards ablaze with red flowers,

Heineken boxes, a Bangladeshi star with blue eyes,
peacocks, pink fans of filigree. The drivers sweat

and strain in their plaid *lungis,* and each face
seems to say *Allah takes and Allah*

gives. A woman breathes into her green shawl
against the dust on the road's median. A man

with a plaid scarf (surplus from The Gap)
slaps the rump of a passing gray car

as though it's a horse or a dog. You are there, too,
your maroon sleeves begin to stick

despite your deodorant. Under your *orna,*
a laminated map and digital camera

cradled in your lap. One strand of silver
wiry by your ear. Bits of children's songs

snag in your windpipe. Other words surface:
sweatshop and *abject poverty,* and you let them.

They mix with the low rumbling that began
on the plane, *m*s and *b*s tumbling, amplified

in the streets: the rickshaw bells' light metal,
the nasal peal of horns. On this continent,

the ocean's giant tongue has swept away
miles of coastline, and bodies flood the water.

Dust sifts into your lungs and sinks—feline,
black, to remain long after you leave.

I

From the Fatwa Series

On my drive to work, I dial three time zones
to seek counsel on dreams in which *two pills*
grew from my hands. Didn't know which to take.
And then the house exploded.
                              In my home,
dreams were the only holy text we shared,
rendered more clearly than our gold-leaf Koran
or muezzins hawking "no God but God"
like wailing auctioneers.
                              House rules: nightmares,
once told, won't come true. I still call my sisters
at odd hours, states apart, to explain
you swam behind me in the water but
you couldn't keep up, or *your fingers*
fused into ladles.
                              Just the other day,
I called my dad to say, *you served a dish*
that took eleven years to make. Steamed greens.
We ate them. Good or bad, he asked, laughing.
Good, I said. But I meant the vegetables.
Didn't tell him how his voice trembled
as he served us, how his hands shook at his plate.

Thinking of His Jaywalking Ticket While Boarding a Plane at SFO

Years ago, he refused to pay it. He said
city officials painted a crosswalk
straight from police department
to donut shop. His refusal

won't land him in Gitmo.
He's not in the slammer.
And this is not the Texan town where
your sister's called *another dirty Mexican*

waiting in the ER all night with cold
coffee and a feverish child. Not *spray-of-glass-*
at-the-back-of-your-sundress
Ohio where you once

fed stale bread to ducks.
He's seated at your side,
elbow to elbow, prepared
to grow slack-jawed over books.

Years ago, he'd found no
safe way to walk from that bus stop,
no path for the workers
waiting to dash through traffic gaps,

no end to his disbelief when the officer
issued a ticket for crossing four lanes.
Years ago, and still
you feel fear's pin-prick

when you hear the words
alien, raid. Detained. Deported.
The plane seats fill and fill
while, in your mind, his seat

empties and empties—as your mouth empties
and your lungs empty each time you hear
we need to ask a few questions.
No one has approached

your aisle, for now. You're safe
to begin your own
cross-examination:
Which swallowed Arabic vowel

will trap him this time?
Which sandpaper *Anwar?*
Which fish-bone *Khalid?*
You'd like to tease and say,

*Mothers, do not name
your sons Mohammed.* But
you do not joke anymore.
You don't joke about anything.

What the Fortune Teller Said

Last night I dreamt
                    of the book of Genesis
of pharaohs and golden
light and loveliness. Then
                        the boardwalk
splintered in our throats
the unspoken
reeling us
            through another bucket
of quarters—ten or twenty bucks.

Inside we spin for hours
                        a dream sweet
as a fruit's most rotten flesh
is sweet.

On the drive home
                the skyline teases
        bridges grow filament-thin
while marshlands spread open

        nothing more.
At the roadside
        milkweed pods
                        silken tufts
the broken shell
            in our hands.

Voltage

My sandals gather dung in the fields—
my heels caked with dirt, collecting
a wildness. But my cousins' laughter
is milky, sweet, and rich, a gift
I can't refuse—like their *cha*—nor drink
completely. Their kindness leaves me
somehow bereft. They offer
buttered biscuits, heave a dusty
album from a shelf, show me
photos my parents must have sent
when I was young. I hardly know
myself. The kids, no matter
what their age, dote on me, dressed
today in their finest fabrics. I see
them learning care, learning kindness,
young men with boyish smiles
offering *dal,* eager to hover
by my chair. I see my father there
before power came to the villages:
with his mother, father, with steaming
plates of rice, their faces softened
by a radiance, lamps they called
hurricanes. But we've appeared
too late. Three buzzing bulbs illuminate
our plates.
                    We're offered swan.
My father protests: *I won't*
eat a creature so beautiful.
I chew the sinewy meat, imagining
her slenderness, not pure
white but cross-hatched at her neck.
Before we leave, an aunt
drapes her shawl around my

back, saying *think of me*
when you wear this, a woman
whose shoes remained fresh, untouched
as we walked the winding fields. I press
her hands, kiss her owl-eyed child.

Mississippi Delta

The only laundromat is on the white side
of town, so you wash your clothes
in the hotel sink. Below your window,

an industrial park flat as a runway,
scattered with rocks and shattered glass.
Even the prison, you hear,

folded a few years ago. The best jobs
are north of here: *50 miles, Tunica,*
riverboat pay. By moonlight you drove

that open stretch of 61 where
a stranger warned, *don't pull off the road.*
Because the yoghurt and salad

you'll find on sale are a week
into rotting. Because the cashier
won't return your change

or smile. Because the boy who stops
by your window in the parking lot
is no more than nine. He asks

for change to buy a burger
and you worry that some teens
put him up to it. Alone beyond

the pale circumference of lights,
you whisper, *I'm sorry, sweetheart. No.*

Dear Masoom

We are happy to hear
you have electric in your home,
that the pipes by each window
keep you warm. What a kind
government to provide
milk, butter, and cheese.
Arey, if only ours would do the same—
but it can't keep the trash
off the capital's streets.
We hope you and Shilpa are well.
The little ones, send them
our love. Please come home soon.
Appa would like to see you
before she dies.

The blankets you mailed
are quite fine—Maya and I share
one, as I gave mine
to Appa. She coughs and rasps
all night despite the ginger tea.
I can hardly sleep
for the noise. Appa is growing older,
you know, so the monsoons make her
wheeze, the dust makes her wheeze,
weather changes make her wheeze.
I hear her now as I sit
wrapped in the one blanket
Maya and I share.

Brother, we are well
in most regards. We are keeping
warm in the sweaters you mailed
last year, the dry season upon us

already. At night the chill could break
your bones. Just last week
the *shim* vine's beans grew as shiny
as eggplant, but now the jinn
rise in the fields.

Halloween

Our spooks are harmless: ceramic
pumpkins grimace
at doorsteps, plastic
cats lunge
from hedges. Ghosts
dangle from my neighbor's
tree, each cotton swatch bound
around a foam globe
with string. They sway
from branches in the breeze with
cinched necks like hanged men,
or the hooded.

The moon's a chlorine stain, giant
cipher. The children's shouts grow
soft along our road. Who haunts
my door now? A vision—a child
from Sudan. Age three, a girl.
Who flinches in the shadow
of any man. Who bears
ruptures no healer can fix
by solder or stitch.

Dhaka Bazaar before Departure

The women slip
glass bangles over my wrists—
even the narrowest, impossible
rings. My sister hisses, *they know*
by your walk you aren't
from here, never mind
your dark hair, your skin. I've worn
a dozen of my mother's gold bands—
eased on with dabs of Vaseline—
but still, I'm filled with disbelief
as they coax glass over my skin.
Bird-like, twittering,
they beseech me in Bengali: *Appa,*
so beautiful. And how can I refuse?
I do not buy the bracelets
simply for their shine,
but for these women:
not much older than I and
wizened, with voices calling out
to me. For them, I want to strip
my pockets clean.

Ahead, my mother rummages for
bootlegged CDs, multi-film
DVDs. She haggles, but now, less
stern, she shrugs, saying, *I can't justify*
another taka for me.
                          In customs, thieves slip
gifts from my suitcase. We sleep
on the plane while each keepsake
is resold to the marketplace. Stateside,
we find there's nothing left
to steal or own but the train's

midnight screech. Nothing, that is,
but these bangles. I'm empty-handed.
I can forget what I've heard and seen.
I can free myself from this glass.

The Other Side

(on Gauguin)

What brings you to the clearing? Our fruit,
our flesh—is it as you imagined?
Ah, but the fruits you paint are brighter, bigger
than any we find here, the blooms bolder
and more varied. This tree, not so dark as black-
skinned avocado; more like green young breadfruit.
Sweeter in the mind than on the tongue, as they say.

Do we seem untroubled? Do we seem pure?
I know what the others say: that you left
in Copenhagen a wife, one child
for each finger on your hand. That your hands—
which now, with care, place an urn
in my palm—once bloodied her face. Or twice.
But who am I to judge? Lounging here all day
with the others, clustered like tree snails.

And her flesh, her face—is it as you thought?
You know she doesn't like that dress, the one
with blanched banana leaves flanking
her neck. That collar—see how stiffly she sits.

When your boat first approached I thought
a white bird was rising from the water—at a distance
and in the sun, it seemed a great chunk of salt
to wipe away my mother's fever. Everyone said,
here comes another, this one with a brush
instead of a book, or rope, or whip.

After the Argument

there's no apology, only a pink and red cluster of nine new flowers in the back yard. Now, her brow creases with the gentle Vs that ducks trail through water. She thinks of Center City: the nights she waited while he hunched over books in a library of troublesome words. The sounds she tried to carry in her mouth at the market, the bus stop, the bank. Some nights he arrived late from his studies, waking her to eat hot pizza, late-night takeout. She recalls the saris he bought for her, hundreds of yards stored in suitcases, one for each day she had been away from home. How he had folded her wedding silk with care on their first night together, how he had prayed and prayed for them before they first shared that bed. Each evening, she would clear the living room before he returned, hiding the paper so he would come, first, to her, to touch his hands to her face.

Small House

Here is the grave of my father's mother
and father. Two oblong mounds of earth:
my sweet unknown. A decade

too late, I stand at the ravine's drying
waters, I hold the lacy yellow flower.
Even in the dry season, the grass

is vibrant, green, checkered with the
haze of mustard. No sound
but open sky and the scattered light

tones of a rickshaw or
two children laughing, splashing
near the water's low edge.

In the quiet current, a bamboo fish net
looms as an art piece,
all mesh and stick. The graves rest

in a raised stone wall that is both
a small house and crumbling foundation.
They tell my father, *she lived on*

waiting to see you. The green and yellow
patches roll into the distance, land
as flat as Ohio where I watched

rows of corn file past from the
backseat. Men and women crouch
or stand among seedlings just like those

who picked mushrooms and tomatoes.
Here, each path through the rice fields
rises in a narrow mound of earth

like the sacred serpent grounds
of the Adena, each muddy seam
guiding my step. I hover

for a while over the trail's
raised Braille to learn
what the land will say, put my

cheek to the grass and listen.

Overheard

Who's here to receive me
after so many years? I blame
the doctors, not the cancer
that took her. And you ask me, now,
why I cannot sleep? Nor eat—
cream of coconut, curried cabbage,
fried eggplant, nothing. I walked
to the pond where we once
skipped stones but the fish float,
having died long ago.

Here's the room in which a thief
grabbed my sister's arm
one night when her wrist
went limp near the windowsill.
He must have seen her bangles
flash. I clutched the long thick braid
of her hair after that. Night after
night, it was a bristled rope to keep
me from the underworld.

Advice

A child enters water
        first, then a name and then
a body—a history.

She needed avocado
        flesh, almonds, and
milk, more milk

than any student funds
        could have supplied
(when a half-cup fed

both mother and growing
        child). Her children
grew round and gold,

fed by another country's
        butter. When they, too,
grew heavy

she instructed them
        daily: three full cups
and lots of rest.

They did not guess
        she ever carried anything
but a worried

look on her face. Or that
        for a cup of rice
a local midwife had delivered

each one of them,
        delivered from water
to breath. What little relief

from the silver pins
        used to stitch
her whole again.

Fugue of New Motherhood

One body must
wane so another
may grow.
That body is mine.

One body must
weaken so another can
thrive. That body
is mine.

One back must
break. One back
must break.
That breaking is mine.

One body must wake
so another
can sleep.
That body is mine.

One body
must sleep.
That sleep
is not mine

but sweet on
the lips of
an infant.
I sleep only

in whatever time is
left once I've studied
his chest for the faintest
rise and fall

of breath.

Grace

My baby's cry is a siren's
wail washing over the city.
Where's the silence

that sleep brings?

When I shower the phantom
cries grow faint, each peal
real or imagined

water-hushed under
the showerhead's shush.

What's the meaning of collapse?

My jaw ratchets when I bite.
Each tooth ground to a nub.
I think of food eaten whole,

the wild animal
I've become. No one numbers
how many failures

are private, how many public.

Who will forgive me if I
act with anything
less than grace?

The body still functions.
He still extracts
what he needs—

my child at my breast:
fleshy, sated.

I churn water to milk,
spin straw into gold.
Weep, weep,
good little machine.

Roulade

The rain's roulade against the roof
will wake her, not the muezzin's call
to prayer at dawn, though she'd been drawn
to it one night in her father's village,

cousins arm in arm down a moonlit road,
filmi style, romantic. Earlier that day,
the boys had shared one piece of paper
as though it were a sheet of gold.
                                    Back in the city
young uncles asked about the countryside,
laughing in her face as she answered *ducks,*
horses, when she should have said *the rice paddies*

quilted the fields by the river or *the breeze*
filled my lungs with song. Mute, monolingual,
she snapped photos of her grandmother
until she smiled, one white lash

at her eye like a snowflake.

Alpana

Sister, let's get my story
straight: one hand stains
your shirts so the other
can place rice
on my child's plate.
I either sweat here
or under a stranger's
weight. So when you
boycott a storefront
you'll need a louder
roar to scare off
our global predator—
let's call him
Mr. Sweetmeat,
from the land of milk
and money, selling
garments stitched
by a woman
like me. This is no
alpana: lovely dust
arranged and
erased in a week.
This work means
my child and I eat.

Meet your new-world
artisan. And before Boss-man
will declare, "Honey, let's
get you a chair, fix these
doors, give you
breaks, and—
really—pay you
more," he'll shut

down and begin again on
the other side of town.

The cloth is cut. The needle
waits. Take the blood from our
thumbs to lace your suits
and skirts. Someone always hungers
to enter the broken gate.

Invitation

Join me at the desk where
you sit in the dim photograph
smoothing your black hair
into a bun, eyelids dark with kajal,
sari draped across your chest.

But surely the heat will
kill us. Our bodies won't
withstand the water, the sun.

Walk stories with me: the dirt path
to the midnight bazaar, where
merchants open stalls
for Eid, selling bangles
and milky-sweet *shondesh.*

On asthma days, breath comes
as though through a sieve.
The winter winds are full of dust.

We'll paddle the silver pond
where you once swam,
to the bamboo mat where
your mother sits in this
photo: slim arms. White sari.

In every paper, news
of the dengue fever.
And my mother, gone.

Let's wander the college halls where
you first traded letters, take a long
cool drink from the jug
outside the classroom while
students squirm in the heat.

Now, an election year,
mobs rise in a cyclone's wave,
so much political unrest.

We'll sit in the verandah's
clean symmetry,
the evening-cooled porch
filled with cousins, mango
trees heavy with fruit.

The porch is boarded up now,
the house, long since divided
into smaller dwellings.

I thought you'd sail
into that sea with
me, into the water
hanging at the horizon
like a pale slice of slate.

So long since I stopped
sending crisp blue airmail.
And my mother, gone.

I knew little of the distance
between Bryn Mawr
and Brahmanbaria, of Chillicothe
and Chittagong, nothing
of your hemisphere, your heartland.

How we climbed as children
to gather green coconut,
its sweet soft flesh.

Come: let's drive. We'll ride
the swells along the road
to the park, the bumps
next to trees whose paved roots
still nudge.

Petition

What god will catch me
when I'm down, when I've taken
sufficient drink to reveal
myself, when my words are little
more than a blurring
of consonant and vowel?

I'm drunk on spring:
branches of waxy leaves that
greet me at my driveway,
a family clutching
trays of sweets.
How can I sing of this?

If I cannot sing, then
make me mute. Or lend me
words, send me
the taste of another's prayer,
cool as a coin
newly minted on the tongue.

Ghazal

It's wine I need. Is it a sin to have another?
No harm in merlot, no harm in another.

In Ramadan, we'll break our fast with dates and wine—
Must we pray in one room and dance in another?

Crushed blossoms at the end of the summer, teach me
how to coax nectar from the bloom of another.

Burned rice on the stove again—what's to love
but my imperfections—you'll forgive me another.

Butter by a kettle always melts, warns the proverb.
Heated, greased, we slip one into the other.

When, inexplicably, you enter my prayers,
I hear messages from one god or another.

Me encanta cantar, cuando estoy sola, en el carro.
My mother tongue dissolves. I speak in another.

Heart-thief, enter the fields like a woman in love,
vase in one hand, shears in the other.

II

Southeastern Ohio

In stuffy gyms that passed
for mosques, my sisters and I
parroted words without grace:
*Allah hu akbar. Salaam
alaikum.* Then the prayer-song broke
and we mimicked instead
lyrics thrumming from
somebody's Walkman: *I want
your sex.* The station wagon crawled
from house to house where
driveways spilled
with brown kids, where a friend
flashed her *thabees* as though
casting a hex.
                    In another country,
we'd have fasted and feasted in a
month of sunset meals, wearing
gifts of new dresses. Instead,
I took salt in my mouth
with our neighbors, brothers
from Egypt who passed the ball
and dribbled and spit all month
on the court, avoiding
their own saliva.

Turn

At the field's perimeter
        frog eggs churned

to tadpoles. Grass
        stained our jeans

while wood-scents rose
        among rocks

and trees. We found
        pollen-breath,

nectar-threads, morning
        glory and mint.

Honeysuckle grew suddenly
        in pairs of barrettes

when girls emerged
        from hedges

wearing cotton skirts
        and flowered dresses.

Rumor Had It

she jogged the river trail
      in a sari. Chiffon layers

draping crooked arms,
      atchel whipping

in the wind. White
      running shoes pounding

along the Hocking.
      She blurred

into a mad red
      bird. Through screened

windows I heard a flurry
      of silk or slapping

soles—tried to catch
      a flash of damp

tendrils at her neck. Faceless
      she flew

over houses and fields
      while I searched the sky

for her sweat-soaked sari, longed
      for a glimpse

of her unraveling bun.

Clepsydra

I found sassafras
leaves to float downstream,
mosquitoes on water, shy
plants that shrank at my

touch. I might recall a certain
weight, but it was the sun
on my back—balmy,
almost solid. Or the rocks I

collected in the folds of my
sundress, the hem frayed
because I wore its blue
all summer. Mint

sweetened the air. I heard a low
ripple. Then a Doppler shift
of bees. On the other side
I poked poison sumac, pinched

blades between my thumbs
to slice the quiet
with a resounding bleat.
I struggled to build a dam

with twigs and unsettled
clumps as though
the earth wouldn't heave
silently downstream.

Lightning

She punched
        holes in jar-lids
                for walking sticks
and crickets
        but not for fireflies.

Instead the sidewalk
        became her canvas,
                each bug her paint,
with glowing bellies
        scraped onto pavement.

Lips bitten
        in concentration
                and loose strands
slipping from a jeweled
        clip, she cupped

each yellow bulb
        with tenderness.
                Then the twig,
the precision
        and patience.

Clear Water

I could tangle my fist in her hair
when the sun struck or the mood
struck me, or shove snow
into the warmth between her neck
and sweater. These were mine.
I remember the time she told
our mother she wanted to *break glass,*
how they rode together to the tracks
so she could fling bottles
into the dark. Now she is a rock
worn smooth with worry, and I am clear
water. But I am not clear water.
And I was not forgiven. I listen
to her child's voice until I grow sick:
Hello. Mom. Hello. Mom. Another message
the scratch of the phone kicked
along pavement at 4th and King,
but they don't live in my city.
When he says *car* and *gas station*
I think of the fumes, how she lowered
the back windows to inhale
when our parents stopped to refuel.
What else but this place between burn
and breeze? I wanted to stop her
the day she entered the woods.
Like the stray we couldn't coax
from the branches once the blizzard hit,
it's cold out here come inside
her face held a wildness I recognized:
bewilderment, the certainty of getting lost.

Amateur's Guide to Divination

The water
        was no obstacle:
my feet

were not mine,
        a matter of
angels.

Could I walk across—
        bodiless?
Blue pond

became sky:
        porcelain, cloudless,
Ohio, open, mine.

One silver sphere
        floating toward center—
oracular,

something that spoke
        if spoken to.
Mosquitoes buzzed:

interference
        in reception.
But I heard

the call. I grasped
        the strange beginnings
when blue gills

shimmered,
        breaking
the glass meniscus.

Carnival

We'd only begun to detect
the air was full of tricks
if a woman could,
in a man's hands, disappear.

The boys who manned the carousel
punched each other's arms
when we dropped
hot coins into their greased palms.

We took a whirl. We preened like
park birds, creatures who
feed from strangers' fingertips.
We took a crack at the vanishing

act with the lunches
we packed—cucumbers, yoghurt.
We could stage
our own departures.

Weren't our bodies
meant to be flat?
Those women onstage,
the wisps they became—

they infused our hair
with a form of belief.
Carolina jasmine
choked the breeze

while magicians produced
rabbits from hats, doves
where there'd been none.

Picasso's *Self-Portrait in Blue Period,* 1901

At twenty: haggard,
lean as a stray, someone
I cross the street to avoid at night
even as I notice
                   pink lips, blue
hollowed cheeks. By now, we've both lost
friends we won't recover. Huddled
in his navy coat, he watches from
room to room. His grief, mine—
eyes two sunken tombs.

Dustcover

Fresh grief, when I find another poet
has died. In my ignorance, I grieve
as though each loss is new, and I, a friend
at the graveside. As we leave, they too leave.

Who has died? In my ignorance, I grieve
for the old poets, who left me too soon
at the graveside. As we leave, they too leave.
Weather-worn, world-weary. Weakened, I croon

for the poets who have left me too soon.
Between hardbacks, at libraries, I weep.
Weather-worn, world-weary, weakened: I croon.
It's as though I've woken from some great sleep

at libraries, between hardbacks, and I weep,
now disenchanted, now unswayed.
It's as though I've woken from some great sleep
and long to return to it, betrayed—

now disenchanted, now unswayed
by what I learn, by those who raise me.
I long to return to them, betrayed
as I am: I need their words to see.

By what I've learned, by those who've raised me
I hope to do right—hardened, imperfect
as I am. I need their words to see
what we've loved, and what we've wrecked.

I hope to do right. Hardened, imperfect—
I still hear echoes in every sun-baked urn
of what we've loved, or what we've wrecked.
I let the words bear down and burn.

I hear echoes in every sun-baked urn
of fresh grief, when I find another poet.
I let their words bear down and burn
as though each loss is new, and I, a friend.

Qawwali

Because you were schooled in no
instrument and I could carry

no tune, there would be no
music between us, not even

at the place of oracle, no matter what
story the flames told. And so I

wasted, desired by none,
whatever beauty

faded, shades lost
to gray. Each feature cracked.

So let me join the fakirs who
beg at the roadside, singing

hymns to Allah, eyes
bleached by the sun.

This is my crooked *qawwali*,
an introductory wail, my vocal

improvisation. With jasmine strands
tangled at my neck, I'll lose myself

in the traffic's vortex,
mehndi marking my palms

like a scar or a scab.
I'll learn the patience of sorry

angels who stand by and let it
happen, haloes nothing more

than a scratch in paint.

Fever

so remote   you can't be sure

    how long   until help arrives   where no car or van

can reach you   in time   where babies

    aren't named   for days   can't be sure

how long   they'll survive   my nani died

    of a flu   my mother couldn't   see her

now she's ready   handful of pills

    at the slightest sign   of fever

I have gone there   through potholed roads   bones rattled

    rattled faces   unmistakable gesture   of hand

to mouth   her smeared lipstick   ten years old

    wasn't sure   who was who   palms darkened

at the side of the road   places   I might have been   born

    places   I might have called   home   even the river   burns

Josiah

Didn't want to see his tiny body,
       the perfect pearls of toes, but

you needed to reveal the photo,
       to say *he was mine.* I carry him

with me now as I watch a couple
       walk in the rain, how the man pinches

loose cloth at her elbow, not holding
       her hand, or when a boy sits

at the next table, his reflection in the glass
       so solid and resolute that

for long moments I cannot place
       him, neither here under lamps with

a mug of steam, nor there on the street
       where teenagers walk

through him, spinning their umbrellas,
       the dome of town hall

a painted egg, muted shades of blue
       and gold. Tulips, wet newspaper,

school kids with cell phones.
       Now that he's gone

I want to believe in a place
       of light, fat fists

to hold him beyond
      the tooth of his

gravestone, where dogwood
      trees will soon turn

to snow, handfuls of white
      petals framed by the window.

Dust and Ashes

I have seen the spiked lavender, sage,
spiny as a sea creature, and felt
neither dumb joy nor bitterness.
Mustard flowers in hills as
high as a horse, and I hold
no pain. Poppies glow
in scattered patches by the road
and I'm neither drawn nor
repelled. No longer turned

brittle by the shushing of jacaranda
nor by the hot, dry scent of summer.
I live there no more. I live now
at the well-bottom, mouth
open to catch copper coins.

The Gardener's Concession

I'm quick to pick the bud
with the weed.
In daylight I face

accusatory veins
and uprooted hyacinth
shoots. The blameless

talc of lavender
dusts the ivy leaves.
Spring is ripped

from tulips.
                    And so,
destroyed: both

what's plucked and
what we reap
while I seek earth

so deep it holds
no bloom
as though I

could divine
the loam from which
we're made—quarry

the clay or
at least discover
the dirt that holds

our imprints when
we shape it
with our hands.

Return

City, I've tried to love your gray-veined streets
that wind through grayer hills, bits of driftwood
stagnant downstream, steel bridges, your concrete.
I've paced hollows, your twisting neighborhoods:
trestles tucked away near mills, now quiet,
plastic bags that sprout like strange white flowers,
an orange haze not quite the sun. Cardboard
houses crushed into hills, slow heat, hours

pressing into me. No town of my own,
just this confluence of leaden waters—
Monongahela: slate. Allegheny: bruise.
Bridges lit up in bright spokes of moonstone
seem to point home, but among splinters,
where in each river does the water move?

Witching Hour

Tonight, I will learn the names of trees
that flank my street and chant
in invocation: eucalyptus, gingko,

sycamore, beech. I'll speak
three languages of longing: *lebu, limón,*
limoni. But in the witching hour

I'm too tired to cast my spells, while the wind
spins a stranger at my door—a pillar
of dust, less particle than air,

someone I cannot grasp, or when I do,
who disappears.
                                        Tea-stained clouds spill
around the moon—another mess

I've gotten into. Forgive my insolence;
forgive me sun, moon,
for the words

I haven't spoken, or intend to soon.
I've tried to claim that $E + H = L$
and therefore, we exist, and therefore,

we love. But there is no math
to our names. If I didn't heed
the heart's complaint when I first

felt it, when something shuddered
from my chest—not like an angel,
no. Not a bird of paradise.

I am the bird who breaks her beak
against the glass, but there is no past
to recover. Instead, I'll remember

the future. Let's start with a place
where I've never been.

Fable

Soon, I will arrive at a house aglow
with lights and an endless meal, plate
after steaming plate to feed all
who enter. And if my feet are muddy,
my hands cold; if I have stumbled,
as I will tell you, now, I have stumbled—
with my faith returned to me like a pouch
of broken bones—I found my face
among the villagers. I haven't walked
here alone. And now the night holds my name
in the thicket, the sky the ribbed scales
of a fish, phosphorescent, backlit.

Behind the house, I'm told, there's a river
full of minnows, now drawn together, now
drawn apart. Beyond that is a woods
dark enough for disappearing,
and at each root, a dirt
soft enough to knead.

The 18th-Century Weavers of Muslin Whose Thumbs Were Chopped

(after Agha Shahid Ali)

They became extraneous.
By some brutal magic
those who spoke *angrezi*
fashioned rice into cotton, made

slaves of them all.

⁓

Tonight
you're bewitched by a market
full of visions. Lit candles
wink and warn as rickshaws

approach, revealing pyramids
of oranges, drums of green
coconut, a man with pale
cabbages piled on top

of his head.

⁓

What you've heard
of the weavers is no alchemy. It's true:
they could have woven
a cloth as fine as mist.

Beyond silk. Beyond gossamer.
Twenty yards in a matchbox
like folded air. Or fifteen
through a golden band, diaphanous.

⁓

Later,
          will their stories vanish, too?
No traveler, no trader will recall
their wizardry among jute
rugs on the street, silken saris,

notched sugar cane, or tea leaves
that crumble—while absence
pulses like the phantom
thumbs. *Hush child, my eyes*

are so tired.

⁓

          Beyond the half-
glow of the city, a pond stagnates
full of plastic bags where someone
bathes his feet and dreams of

braiding his lover's hair.

Cathedral

I take care to pick a seat
untouched by sun to hide
my face from the believers.
In a house of worship where
I've never knelt,
I watch pilgrims press
forward with small donations, touching
wicks to those already lit, adding
heat to the chorus.
I've long wanted to
stand at the altar, to light
my wick with the flame
of another.
I have wanted to sing.

At the Stove-Side

What a thing! She arrives just in time
to slice onions for me, the rice
overflowing with froth at the lid.
The guests were happy with drinks
in hand but soon wanted
more than the *poppadoms* I'd fried.
I was glad when I woke but
sorry all day—she was no longer at my side
while chopping potatoes, stirring the *dal,*
frying seeds as they sputtered.

Now I've burnt this minced garlic, which adds
bitterness no matter how fresh
the vegetables. No matter, as my mother
often said, "No point in pointing
fingers when a mess has been made—I'm the one
who'll have to clean it up."
She watches me always, I think—
especially in April, when crocuses
poke through and die before you blink.
I lost her twenty years ago this week.

Mother

That I could rub this belly and conjure
        a child before you go: golden bangle

on her fat wrist, saffron highlights in the sun.
        She won't know she has your half-playful, half-

cruel knack for a joke, the same glossy hair
        that slips from a bun. Deft hands that shape foil

into swans or pull tomatoes from vines
        with gentle pressure. Later, she'll feel your absence,

too. She won't know that, years before
        you'd understand *malaria* or *dengue fever*

or neighbors gathering in lines to give blood,
        you sailed your road by boat

when the first floods rippled at your door.
        How you and three brothers gazed at the fish—

mercurial flashes. Light in the dark.
        She won't hear the old stories: names

I can't remember, places I've never been.
        You'll return to her in the dryness

of bay leaves, the mingled scents
        of pepper dust and pine. She'll measure spices

into pots in all the right combinations.
        It will take a lifetime to get it right.

The Map of Another Country

Were there a way to strip us
clean of desire, how free we'd be,
released—

the rain's grit or
prophecy no longer
plain. But our skin is scarred

by its own burn—
by a blessing; a curse.
See our birthmarks

splattered across backs or
calves: the map of another
country. Inkblots marking us

desirous of everything
we can see or touch—persimmons
bursting in alleys, crushed,

slick with their own juices.
Each merchant's pyramid of
cinnamon, lips laced with sweet

dust—will this craving
choke
or sustain us?

New Year

Last night something
         tunneled through the elms.

But at sunrise,
         I found just white light

biting my eyelids, salt
         rubbed on a wound.

Batons of ice
         fell from power lines,

soundless but still emphatic.
         Then the rain

churned the snow to soap
         scum, waxing cars with

winter's lichen, patchy
         in the strange

uneven fur of newborns.
         And still, I was childless.

One cardinal
         lodged on a branch:

a blood-drop
         striking water

before the slow dispersion.

In Brussels I Learn to Love

the rain, the way wet streets
grow dark and expectant, mercury
puddles looking back at me,
each silver building

shivering in its own height.
A dampness in my toes, I arrive
by train armed with practiced
phrases: *s'il vous plaît, je voudrais.*

Tonight, the world feels
clean and alive: lush fields
crouching under a steamy
milk of fog, blanched sheets

flapping in the wind. A stump
shoved along a fence
like a bull's flank. Under my feet,
anywhere, the River Senne

pulses below cement and stone,
bricked away like a midnight
demon, an ink-dark vein
that gave the city life but

could not sustain it. Above,
in this world, rain-slapped streets
glisten with candle-lit restaurants.
I buy scraps of lace and

tissue-wrapped chocolates, the taste
of a new language
sweet and unwieldy
on my tongue. At the cathedral,

I fumble with my phrasebook,
foolish and free with the shopkeeper—
her toothy smile and translucent skin
framed by a drab scarf, both of us

laughing at our limits, then
humbled by the student who
offers to translate: a Canadian
girl with wild curls, a black jacket,

and a stinging sense of fluency.
The bus coughs and swallows
blue hats, striped scarves, and
backpacks through one

swift door. A rain hesitates
at my shoulders, so fine
it feels like snow.
The engine's roar fills

me, fills each slow traveler:
the woman with crooked bits
of straw teeth, the man who stands
alone on cement islands, selling

newspapers to the wind.
Silent fires blaze behind
glass, the pubs' facades
encrusted with statues and

cannonballs. On the indigo
road back to the countryside,
wildflowers unfold petals and
open their small dark throats.

Venice during an Election Year in the US

We learn what we love
        when it's half-sunk:
a ship's hull slipping
        from vision, just a tip

visible to remind us of its
        hidden bulk.
Entire cities sink
        without solution.

A piazza's bricks
        succumb to floods.
Tourists. Cellists. Pigeons.
        There's silver water

putrid with fish-stink,
        littered paper
lapping in canals. Wilted lilies.
        Each day bears the pull

of a dead weight.
        To our left,
a bobber shudders
        on a cast line

before it dips
        and disappears.
To our right
        someone's trawl breaks.

Limoni

When the day's heat bakes
        our clothes, when

our patience crumbles
        with monuments and ruins,

we'll desert history
        to study our own lives

through sea salt, lemons, anchovies.
        White grapes and wine.

All shades of blue
        on the Ligurian. We'll stagger

from the train wanting
        to be revived

by the coast, grains of sand.
        Chiaroscuro and *carugi*.

We'll keep time, then, by nothing
        but nail-notch, a cut

in dimpled rinds. Let's find
        a scent to make us want

to live: sun-fed, needy.
        Flesh at the point of breaking.

Jinn

My name comes to me like an angel.
—Tomas Tranströmer

I walk into the wind
           any excuse
to stray before the storm   gusts
pressing into me   giant hands
against my form. This was proof

that I existed.
          Spring, and I'm
melancholy—backlit
blue sky
     full moon
to remind me.   Waft of chlorine
    a pool
shaped like a kidney.
         The trees
are my keeper   their rustle
    of history   yet

I wind one hair
        around a knuckle
just as my mother
taught me. And then this—
           a gift—
my name
       returned to me
wrapped in a voice I recognize

                  a sound the wind
will steal or lift
                        the way
the night pulls a web
from the water.
                        I'd like to think
it's one beloved on the way
          to another
but who can name
          what twitches in the leaves

or what's drawn from my body
like a vapor
          like a kiss?

Evening in Mendocino

You're blanketed in the
smell of sea kelp, plant
that moves like animal.

Who wouldn't believe
in mermaids? The ocean
is lonely. Forget

long walks at sunset, etc.
Something here grows
ripe. Something grown

from salt. It could wrap
you in strands
so soft you would gladly

give in. Relinquish
your name, your story,
your life. Then sink

to the root of it, anchor
yourself to one water-
darkened rock. Surrender

to sound. Let sunlight
become a memory,
barely recognized or felt.

Looking for Astronauts

but we haven't found any, just two stars
emerging to the east of the Jungfrau,
or a paraglider's afterimage
suspended in air, a swatch
of purple silk. His knees bent
in the moment of takeoff—a beat,
a hesitation—then he leaped
into the stratosphere, sail
shrinking to the size of columbine
against rock and snow. Here at the window—
feet up, coffee mugs—the night drains
all color from our skin
and clothes. Chiaroscuro
to monochrome. You speak slowly, warm
on *limoncino,* a story
about your friend's cousin. I'd like to say
I gave my full attention, but I'm trying
to memorize the snow's glare, your sock
foot on the windowpane, the snuffed
candle's smoke and sweetness.
Above the mountains, the sky
grows deep until each peak
is a ghost patch of bone.

Slicing It Open

I want a fruit that cleaves
         as cleanly as butter, and if
                  its barbed skin

grates my lips with an animal
         scratch, no matter.

Give me one with salmon-
         colored flesh
                  even if its nectars

mask its burrs
         and snares.

Is there no succor
         in the bite that
                  lodges inside,

in the sound
         of a device

that could
         cut me, slowly
                  whirring to life?

In the Echo Chamber

He has already entered our lives
at month five.
Wax-limbed, tethered little flipper
who I'll soon carry on my hip, or
sling onto my chest as though to return
him to his origins. Fern-
fingered fists brushing walls of my uterus
while the two of us
imagine another voice
breaking—another consciousness—
fish-lunged, warm-blooded, numinous
cries
now latent, cushioned by liquid.
Little squid,
born into trinity
even when they cut you free.

Solstice

The fog casts its net
       over everything: cinnamon

branches, bone pavement.
       Milkweed deepens
           to indigo.

A flush of light brings
       the angles of your face

close to me. I rise to find
       jackets strewn
           across the couch,

cords curled under the table.
       A blood-orange

wisp of color in my tea.
       The bed covers become
           a version of myself:

softer, crumpled, still warm.
       Outside, someone

has strung tiny bulbs
       over brick.
           A leaf's three points

blur into the sidewalk.
       As I enter the cobalt

chill of twilight
    the air carries
        faint smoke,

burning paper, leaves.
    The night grows and

grows until it swallows
    the day. It obscures
        my shadow, and hides my face.

Translating Tagore

Mother bird, even you knew,
        were you to chew each word
to place tenderly in my mouth,

I still would not taste
        the sweetness. Not *his love*
                is a blossoming lily or *her wishes*
                        washed away in the waters.

Not like you, your eyes searching
        skyward for a parallel term, lips
pursed around the plush sounds—

each poem possessing
                your body while every word
        caught in my throat
like a *cattah.*

Been speaking in tongues again.

        In sleep, I read the twists
and turns of text, a curlicued Braille,

tracing membrane pages and thinking
        this is where it says
                there was a boy with a name like a fruit

or *her eyes were the color of tamarind.*

Dust Catcher

Unlike you, I haven't yet chosen
the objects for my tomb. My chest
is a trash heap: copper coils and rail ties,
and so many pieces of flint. I've gathered
tungsten and filament—anything that conducts
the heat. Undone, again, when the healer
brings her cart of magic, I buy pyrite
and strands of tiger's eye. All songs
of the mystics. But when is the moment
of alchemy, when each artifact is extracted
from me, one clean scarab in place of the heart?

Jackfruit

(for my mother)

It's taken so long to come home. Skin
sliced in your sister's kitchen, the stink and
burst of flesh, something sweet but

dank with time. The open wound spills.
We bite giant prawns that glow pink
on our plates, then climb to rooftop

views: crooked buildings, Dhaka's jagged
teeth. Bikes churn up dust from beneath
and I feel a great coil unwinding.

Snake-charmed, mesmerized. I chant
my cousins' names as a spell or charm:
Ushmeela. Rashed. Ivy. The gems

of small nieces a nursery rhyme:
Annono, Lavonno, Mo. They paint
looping patterns onto my hands

in maroon veins of mehndi.
We lean by potted sprigs
of henna and cool our feet

on cement. Uncles bring
lemonade, tell stories
of the skyline, smoke

cigarettes. Your sister refused
to leave, so the city piles its
bricks at the base of her door:

industry, haze, noise.
Through traffic-lava,
flats of pipes and giant bolts

rattle past on rickshaw floats.
The vendor's call for *shrimp fish*
is a cry of jubilation, ricocheting

through mud and stone.
For this while, we are shirts
on a clothesline: clean, dry, free.

We toss roasted nuts as hot
as the ones
on the Jersey coast

you'll still drive hours
to eat. You say they
taste better by the sea.

Notes

The book's epigraphs come from the following sources:
   Agha Shahid Ali: *A Nostalgist's Map of America*
   Elizabeth Bishop: *The Complete Poems, 1927–1979*

"Southeastern Ohio" takes a line from a song by George Michael.

   thabees: hollow pendant that bears a prayer or blessing

"Fever" takes its form and title from a poem by Rick Barot.

"Fable" borrows a phrase from Su Tung-P'o: "dirt soft enough to knead."

"The 18th-Century Weavers of Muslin Whose Thumbs Were Chopped"

   angrezi: English

"Looking for Astronauts" takes its title from a song by The National.

"Translating Tagore"

   cattah: fishbone, thorn

Acknowledgments

I gratefully acknowledge the editors of the journals below for publishing the following poems, which sometimes appeared in different forms and/or with different titles.

Blackbird: "Ghazal," "The Map of Another Country," "Qawwali,"
    "Mother," and "Roulade"
Born Magazine: "Dhaka Dust"
Boxcar Poetry Review: "What the Fortune Teller Said"
Catamaran: South Asian American Writing: "Dear Masoom,"
    "Voltage," "Dust Catcher," and "Clepsydra"
Cerise Press: A Journal of Literature, Arts & Culture: "Limoni"
The Collagist: "Venice during an Election Year in the US,"
    "Cathedral," and "Rumor Had It"
Columbia: A Journal of Literature and Art: "Translating Tagore"
Crab Orchard Review: "In Brussels I Learn to Love" and
    "Invitation"
Cream City Review: "Jinn" and "Witching Hour"
diode: "Petition," "Picasso's *Self-Portrait in Blue Period,* 1901," "The
    Gardener's Concession," and "Dustcover"
Drunken Boat: "Dust and Ashes" and "Turn"
The Florida Review: "Clear Water," "Fever," and "Small House"
The Fourth River: "Fugue of New Motherhood," "Amateur's Guide
    to Divination," and "Dhaka Bazaar before Departure"
Fox Chase Review: "Solstice," "Advice," "At the Stove-Side," and
    "Lightning"
The Georgia State University Review: "After the Argument"
Hayden's Ferry Review: "From the Fatwa Series"
Many Mountains Moving: "The 18th Century Weavers of Muslin
    Whose Thumbs Were Chopped"
New England Review: "Thinking of His Jaywalking Ticket While
    Boarding a Plane at SFO"
New Orleans Review: "Dhaka Dust" and "Fable"
The Normal School: "Looking for Astronauts"

North American Review: "Josiah" and "Return"
Pebble Lake Review: "Jackfruit"
Philadelphia Stories: "Slicing It Open"
RHINO: "In the Echo Chamber"
Switchback: "Mississippi Delta" and "The Other Side"

"Invitation" and "The 18th-Century Weavers of Muslin Whose Thumbs Were Chopped" appeared in *Indivisible: An Anthology of Contemporary South Asian American Poetry* (University of Arkansas Press, 2010).

"Mother" appeared in *Thatchwork* (Delaware Valley Poets, Inc., 2009).

"Evening in Mendocino," "Dear Masoom," and "Thinking of His Jaywalking Ticket While Boarding a Plane at SFO" will appear in *Another and Another: Selections from the Daily Grind Writing Series* (Bull City Press).

"Rumor Had It" will appear in *Becoming,* an anthology of women's stories (University of Nebraska).

"Alpana," "Grace," "Carnival," and "Southeastern Ohio" will appear in the *Asian American Literary Review.*

I'm indebted to the editors and staff at Graywolf Press—Fiona McCrae, Jeff Shotts, Steve Woodward, Erin Kottke, Katie Dublinski, Marisa Atkinson, and Leslie Koppenhaver—for guiding me through the publication process with warmth and patience.

Many thanks to Arthur Sze for his generosity and his attentiveness to my work and to Michael Collier for his time and advice.

The following organizations deserve my gratitude: the Bread Loaf Writers' Conference, for awarding a conference fellowship; the Association of Writers & Writing Programs, for granting a Writers' Conferences & Centers Scholarship; and the Carnegie Foundation for the Advancement of Teaching, for providing support for my writing. I'd also like to recognize the Swarthmore Public Library, for the gracious assistance of its staff members.

I am deeply indebted to the teachers and mentors who, through their guidance, kindness, and generosity, have shown me what it means to become part of a community of writers: Judith Vollmer, Shalini Puri, Lynn Emanuel, Toi Derricotte, Lori Jakiela, Rick Barot, David Roderick, Robin Ekiss, Brooks Haxton, Martha Rhodes, C. Dale Young, Reg Gibbons, Yusef Komunyakaa, and Carl Phillips. Many thanks to the faculty and staff of Warren Wilson College's Program for Writers, especially Ellen Bryant Voigt, Pete Turchi, Alissa Whelan, and Amy Grimm.

For their camaraderie, for their support as readers and as friends, I thank Ross White, Lucy Tobin, Tua Chaudhuri, Matthew Olzmann, Scott Challener, Carrie Hechtman, Paul Carroll, Meredith Kunz, Lauren McKinney, and many others—too many to name here but all deserving my gratitude. Special thanks to Desiree Pointer Mace and Denise Delgado for their translation talents. A heartfelt thank you, also, to Ann and Ernie Lieberman.

To my family, for their love, laughter, and encouragement: thank you. And to Shom: my boundless gratitude for showing unwavering faith in me and in my writing, both in spirit and in deed.

DILRUBA AHMED is the author of *Dhaka Dust*, winner of the Katharine Bakeless Nason Prize for Poetry, selected by Arthur Sze and awarded by Middlebury College and the Bread Loaf Writers' Conference. Her poetry has appeared in *Cream City Review, New England Review, New Orleans Review, Pebble Lake Review,* and *Indivisible: Contemporary South Asian American Poetry.* A writer with roots in Pennsylvania, Ohio, and Bangladesh, Ahmed holds a BPhil in Creative Writing and an MAT in Instruction and Learning from the University of Pittsburgh. She is a graduate of Warren Wilson College's MFA Program for Writers and lives in Swarthmore, Pennsylvania, with her husband and her son.

Bread Loaf and the Bakeless Prizes

The Katharine Bakeless Nason Literary Publication Prizes were established in 1995 to expand the Bread Loaf Writers' Conference's commitment to the support of emerging writers. Endowed by the LZ Francis Foundation, the prizes commemorate Middlebury College patron Katharine Bakeless Nason and launch the publication career of a poet, fiction writer, and a creative nonfiction writer annually. Winning manuscripts are chosen in an open national competition by a distinguished judge in each genre. Winners are published by Graywolf Press.

2010 Judges

Arthur Sze
Poetry

Robert Boswell
Fiction

Jane Brox
Creative Nonfiction

Book design by Rachel Holscher.
Composition by BookMobile Design and Publishing Services,
Minneapolis, Minnesota.
Manufactured by Versa Press on acid-free
30 percent postconsumer wastepaper.